SUPER SANDCASTLE
Let's See A to Z

Advisories
to
Zero Degrees

Weather from A to Z

Colleen Dolphin

Consulting Editor, Diane Craig, M.A./Reading Specialist

ABDO
Publishing Company

Published by ABDO Publishing Company, 8000 West 78th Street, Edina, Minnesota 55439. Copyright © 2008 by Abdo Consulting Group, Inc. International copyrights reserved in all countries. No part of this book may be reproduced in any form without written permission from the publisher. Super SandCastle™ is a trademark and logo of ABDO Publishing Company.

Printed in the United States.

Editor: Pam Price
Consulting Editor: Diane Craig, M.A./Reading Specialist
Content Developer: Nancy Tuminelly
Cover and Interior Design and Production: Mighty Media
Photo Credits: Shutterstock

Library of Congress Cataloging-in-Publication Data

Dolphin, Colleen, 1979-
  Advisories to zero degrees : weather from A to Z / Colleen Dolphin.
    p. cm. -- (Let's see A to Z)
  ISBN 978-1-59928-879-6
  1. Meteorology--Juvenile literature. 2. Weather--Juvenile literature. I. Title.

QC863.5.D65 2008
551.5--dc22

2007012156

Super SandCastle™ books are created by a team of professional educators, reading specialists, and content developers around five essential components— phonemic awareness, phonics, vocabulary, text comprehension, and fluency— to assist young readers as they develop reading skills and strategies and increase their general knowledge. All books are written, reviewed, and leveled for guided reading, early reading intervention, and Accelerated Reader® programs for use in shared, guided, and independent reading and writing activities to support a balanced approach to literacy instruction.

About Super Sandcastle™

Bigger Books for Emerging Readers
Grades PreK–3

Created for library, classroom, and at-home use, Super SandCastle™ books support and engage young readers as they develop and build literacy skills and will increase their general knowledge about the world around them. Super SandCastle™ books are part of SandCastle™, the leading PreK–3 imprint for emerging and beginning readers. Super SandCastle™ features a larger trim size for more reading fun.

Let Us Know

Super SandCastle™ would like to hear your stories about reading this book. What was your favorite page? Was there something hard that you needed help with? Share the ups and downs of learning to read. We want to hear from you! Send us an e-mail.

sandcastle@abdopublishing.com

Contact us for a complete list of SandCastle™, Super SandCastle™, and other nonfiction and fiction titles from ABDO Publishing Company.

www.abdopublishing.com • 8000 West 78th Street Edina, MN 55439 • 800-800-1312 • 952-831-1632 fax

This fun and informative series employs illustrated definitions to introduce emerging readers to an alphabet of words in various topic areas. Each page combines words with corresponding images and descriptive sentences to encourage learning and knowledge retention. AlphagalorZ inspires young readers to find out more about the subjects that most interest them!

The "Guess What?" feature expands the reading and learning experience by offering additional information and fascinating facts about specific words or concepts. The "More Words" section provides additional related A to Z vocabulary words that develop and increase reading comprehension.

These books are appropriate for library, classroom, and home use.

A a

Advisory

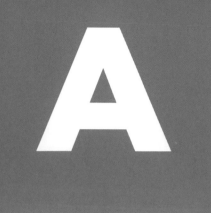

SEVERE WEATHER WARNING

An advisory is a warning.

A weather person gives advisories so we can prepare for bad weather.

Blizzard

A blizzard is a severe storm with wind, snow, and ice.

Winds during a blizzard blow 35 miles per hour or more!

b

B

Blizzards last at least three hours.

Clouds

Clouds are made by ice crystals or small water droplets that form in the sky.

When the droplets in the cloud are too heavy, they fall back down to the earth as rain or snow.

Guess what ? There are billions of water droplets and ice crystals in any one cloud!

Drought

A drought happens when there is little or no rainfall.

A drought causes the land to dry up.

D

d

Evaporate

Mist on this lake is starting to rise before it evaporates.

Heat from the sun causes water from lakes, oceans, and other bodies of water to become a gas. This is called evaporation.

When water evaporates, it becomes invisible.

Flood

When water overflows and covers the land, it is called a flood.

Floods are very dangerous. They damage land and property and can also injure or kill people.

f

F

G g Growing Season

The growing season depends on warm temperatures and enough rainfall.

The growing season is the best time of year to grow most crops.

Hurricane

A hurricane is a storm that forms over tropical waters.

It has strong, rotating winds and moves near coastlines.

Hurricanes cause high waves, thunderstorms, and heavy rainfall.

Hurricanes can also cause tornadoes.

Guess what ?

Winds must reach 74 miles per hour to be considered a hurricane!

I i

ice crystal

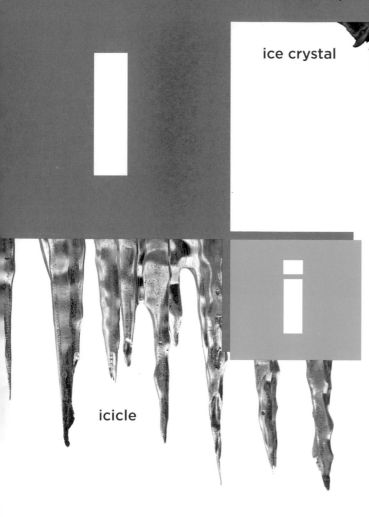

icicle

Ice

Ice is water that has frozen and become solid.

It has many different forms. Two types of ice forms are icicles and ice crystals.

Jet Stream

A jet stream is a narrow band of strong wind located about six to nine miles above the earth.

Major jet stream winds move very fast, usually blowing from west to east.

j

J

Katabatic Winds

K

k

Katabatic winds move downhill. These winds are caused by the ground cooling, which makes the air heavy.

When this happens, the air starts to move very fast down hills and mountains.

Lightning

Lightning is a huge electrical spark in the sky.

Most lightning is formed during thunderstorms.

A lightning bolt heats the air around it to about 50,000 degrees Fahrenheit!

Mud Slide

A mud slide happens when a heavy rainfall makes the soil on a slope very wet.

m

M

The mud can then flow rapidly down the slope.

If large enough, mud slides can cause a lot of damage.

Northern Lights

Northern lights are caused by activity on the sun.

n

N

These solar disturbances cause beautiful, colorful lights to appear in the sky around the North Pole.

Northern lights can be seen most often in the spring and fall in Northern states and countries.

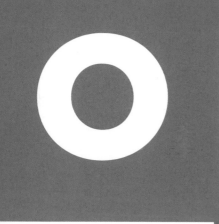

Ozone Layer

The ozone layer starts about 6 to 10 miles above the earth and ends about 30 miles above the earth.

The ozone layer helps protect life on earth from harmful sun rays.

These include ultraviolet rays that can cause sunburn and skin cancer.

18

Precipitation

Precipitation is water that falls from the clouds down to the ground.

Some forms of precipitation are rain, snow, and hail.

Quake

Quake is another name for earthquake.

There are plates under the earth's surface that shift and move.

When this happens, it causes an earthquake.

Earthquakes make the ground shake and can be disastrous.

Rainbow

When light reflects off of water in the air, it creates a rainbow.

r

R

A rainbow is a band of light in the shape of an arc.

Rainbows have red on one edge and violet on the other, with all the other colors in between.

Guess what? Sometimes a second rainbow appears above the first rainbow. This is called a double rainbow!

21

Sandstorm

S

Sandstorms are caused by strong winds over desert areas.

S

Sand is carried up to 50 feet into the air.

A sandstorm can look like a wall of dust.

Tornado

Tornadoes are columns of rotating air that can cause major destruction.

A tornado extends down from a cloud and touches the ground.

The winds in a tornado can reach up to 250 miles per hour.

Guess what ?

Tornadoes can happen anywhere in the world, but they happen most often in the United States.

Ultraviolet Light

The sun gives off ultraviolet light in long, medium, and short wavelengths.

u

UVB, the medium waves, cause health problems in humans.

UVB can damage human skin and eyesight.

Sunblock and sunglasses can help protect us.

U

Volcano

Volcanoes are openings in the earth's surface that allow heat deep inside the earth to escape.

V

V

Ash, gases, and magma are inside volcanoes.

Volcanoes **erupt when pressure forces the magma, ash, and gas to escape.**

W Water

Water is always changing form and moving from the earth to the sky and back to the earth.

The sun heats lakes, oceans, and other bodies of water.

The water then becomes a gas and forms clouds in the sky.

When the clouds are too heavy, the water falls back to earth as rain, snow, or another form of precipitation.

Xeric Climate

Areas in xeric climates receive 10 inches of rain per year or less.

The plants and animals that live in xeric climates have adapted to need little moisture.

X

X

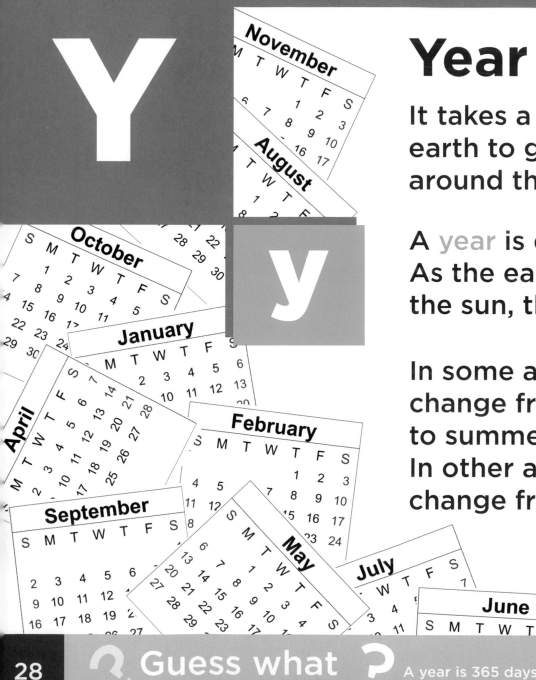

Year

It takes a year for the earth to go all the way around the sun one time.

A year is divided into seasons. As the earth travels around the sun, the seasons change.

In some areas the seasons change from winter, to spring, to summer, to fall.
In other areas, the seasons change from rainy to dry.

Guess what ? A year is 365 days, 6 hours, 9 minutes, and 10 seconds!

Zero Degrees

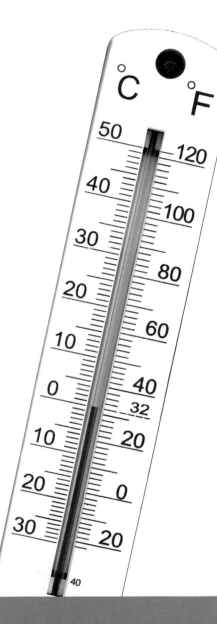

Temperature is measured in degrees.

When it is zero degrees outside, it is very cold!

Water starts to freeze when it is zero degrees Celsius.

Glossary

arc – something that is shaped like a curve or a part of a circle.

cancer – a disease that causes some cells in the body to grow faster than normal and attack healthy organs and tissues.

Celsius – a scale used to measure temperature in the metric system.

climate – the usual weather in a place.

damage – 1) to cause harm or hurt to someone or something. 2) an injury or harm that makes something less useful or less valuable.

dangerous – able or likely to cause harm or injury.

degree – the unit used to measure temperature.

destruction – the state of having been destroyed or ruined.

disastrous – causing or accompanied by disaster.

disturbance – the act of disturbing or interrupting.

Fahrenheit – a scale used to measure temperature in the U.S. customary system.

freeze – to become solid ice from being in the cold.

invisible – not able to be seen.

plate – a large, moveable part of the earth's crust.

reflect – to cause something such as light or sound to change direction.

season – a period of time with a particular type of weather, such as winter or the rainy season.

snow – ice crystals that fall from the clouds to the earth.

storm – very strong winds usually combined with rain, hail, or snow. A storm may also have thunder and lightning.

temperature – a measure of how hot or cold something is.

tropical – located in the hottest areas on earth.

wavelength – the distance from the peak of one wave to the peak of the next wave.

More Weather Words!

Can you learn what these words mean too?

absolute zero	Doppler radar	heat wave	severe weather
air	drizzle	humid	sleet
almanac	dry	inversion	slippery
arid	eclipse	knot	solstice
atmosphere	elevation	lake effect	spring
autumn	environment	landslide	summer
barometer	equator	longitude	thaw
black ice	equinox	meteorology	thermometer
brisk	exposure	mist	thunderstorm
catastrophe	fog	moisture	tsunami
cirrus cloud	forecast	monsoon	typhoon
cold front	frost	muggy	updraft
condensation	global warming	nor'easter	vapor
cumulus cloud	gloomy	overcast	warm
cyclone	gravity	pollutant	warning
damp	gust	prevailing wind	weather vane
degree	hail	radar	weather watch
density	haze	rain	whiteout
dew	heat index	satellite	winter